Medicine Cache Under Lichen

poems by

William Prindle

Finishing Line Press
Georgetown, Kentucky

Medicine Cache Under Lichen

For Rosalyn, who has cheered me along this whole road

And for Tony Russell, Live Poets and Poets at Large, my circles of support

Copyright © 2025 by William Prindle
ISBN 979-8-89990-032-7 First Edition
All rights reserved under International and Pan-American Copyright Conventions. No part of this book may be reproduced in any manner whatsoever without written permission from the publisher, except in the case of brief quotations embodied in critical articles and reviews.

Publisher: Leah Huete de Maines
Editor: Christen Kincaid
Cover Art: William Prindle
Author Photo: Kaya Lee Berne
Cover Design: Elizabeth Maines McCleavy

Order online: www.finishinglinepress.com
also available on amazon.com

Author inquiries and mail orders:
Finishing Line Press
PO Box 1626
Georgetown, Kentucky 40324
USA

Contents

Daylit Revelations
   Finding the Lost Boy Before Dark 1
   A Reunion of Mongrels 2
   A Litany of Saturday Morning Chores 3
   That Comet You Glimpsed 4
   She Sews a Blue Silk Lining 5
   Sunset from the Train South of Manassas 6
   Pages from a Burning Book 7
   Thinking of her Mother 8
   That Hideous Strength 9
   More than the Stock Phrases 10
   Signs of Continued Embodiment 11
   Cups of Comfort 12
   A Spoonful of the Honey 13
   I Lift the Well Cover 14
   Bluejay in Black Walnut Tree 15
   Only When I Looked Down 16
   This Teetering Poem 17
   The Itch of Doubt 18
   The Flutter of an Eyelash 19
   In a Darkened Bedroom 20
   These Holdout Beech Leaves 21
   A Walk into Darkness 22
   I am Just a Flick of a Tail 23
   Your Life is Only This 24
   Loon Requiem 25
   Awakening in an ALS journey 26
   A Drop of Water 27
   Words that Vanish 28
   Lessons 29
   How to Make an Orchestra into a Combo 30
   If I Only Let it Go 31
   Someone You Have Never Seen 32

Ancient Revelations
   Progress Report to Black Elk 35
   Remnant Revenants of Recurrent Dreams 36

Whalebone Necklace 37
Animacy in Wild Strawberry 38
Consonance and Assonance and All 39

News of the Great Turning
Three Lessons in Survival for this Century 43
Planting Words 44
Naked Blind Sweeties 45
Knowing of the Soot 46
A Flat File Across a Mattock Blade 47
Garnets 48
To See the Hummingbird 49
The New Normal 50
This Kitchen Remains Quiet 51
The Bangladesh School of Resilience 52

News of the World
Dispatches from the Levant 55
Lumbering to the Capitol 56
Enthusing with a Glee Undimmed 57
I Pray that Your Ammunition Runs Out before Dark 58
The Truck Driver on my Tail 59
A Field of Cloud Mysteries 60
Stafford's Last Year: Cento 61

Confessional Revelations
That Fluttering Spirit 65
A Poem in which my Grandfathers meet Lorca 66
Parallax Revealed Beneath Princess Pine 67
If Minerva Shrugged 68
What I Didn't Know 69
Mother's Day Pantoum 70
Posthumous Instructions to my Brother Michael 71
My Daughter's New Home 72
What about the Year I Turned 18 73
University Village: Etudes 75
Apologizing to Ferlinghetti 78

An aged man is but a paltry thing,
A tattered coat upon a stick, unless
Soul clap its hands and sing, and louder sing
For every tatter in its mortal dress…

—W.B. Yeats, from *Sailing to Byzantium*

Daylit Revelations

Finding the Lost Boy Before Dark

> *There's a man who walks beside me*
> *He is who I used to be*
> *And I wonder if she sees him*
> *And confuses him with me*
> —Jason Isbell, Live Oak

As a boy no one told him
to wander into the woods
below the field, down through
the laurel grove with its ground
pine, the stream falling over
mossy stone to the river. No one
told him to keep this place as
sacred, or that She kept secrets
there that he alone must keep.

After he got the Crosman pump
action air rifle, a colder energy
came over him. Harder-eyed,
he began shooting squirrels
and birds for no good reason,
including the mallard male
with his iridescent neck that
fluttered broken downriver.

I know that he walks this
ridgeline many an afternoon,
seeking the blessings of
bluebird or pileated or any
created thing. If I hurry
I might overtake him; I
hear Her whispering
that we need to find
the path of restoration
together before nightfall.

A Reunion of Mongrels

Due to this entanglement
stemming from the initial
moment of separation,

my sister's beagle Sprout
lives on in her lab mix Abby
as does my Airedale beagle

Bridget, she who honored
a contract we knew nothing
of but the gravity of which

surrounded us through all
those unsupervised hours
in the laurel woods where

a divinity waited, she who
did not reveal her face to me
until much later, a face that

I hope I will see in the final
hours, in that sweet reunion.

A Litany of Saturday Morning Chores

Let's dispense with formalities.
Let's distinguish ourselves with
      brutal honesty.
Let's gather our vulnerabilities
      by the armful.
Let's make our lives into some
      holy names.
Let's split this rock with a flood
      of tenderness
before that dessicated carapace
      creeps back into place.

That Comet You Glimpsed

Perhaps the best thing about dying
is that there's nothing to pack

and no unpacking, no straps to snap
and unsnap, no point in saying

I'm too tired to do that right now,
no need to act so remote anymore

when all that matters is following
the tail of that comet you glimpsed

transecting your diamond mind.

She Sews a Blue Silk Lining

She leads me down unpaved
uninviting roads.

She beckons left-handed
into the brambled wood.

She demands payment for each
morsel. I cannot resist.

She sews a blue silk lining
in my one remaining coat,

slipping into the sleeve a few
snippets of our old life.

Sunset from the Train South of Manassas

Crepuscular light ignites the treeline;
Birds fly slower than they did at dawn;
Lights in the windows of the lone house
Sparkle as darkness settles on the field.

Dark masses rise in the western sky,
Flamed at their edges as in prophecy.
If I don't hear what God wants by dark,
I'll watch the sky by the lake, and wait.

Pages from a Burning Book

Somewhere on the road ahead
my daughters drive through dusk
into weather patterns I cannot see,

As a northwest wind peels away
the nimbus clouds that pulled my
heart down low all day,

each cloud giving way to something
else, the way book pages curl in censor
fires, until the words are gone,

leaving nothing but the waiting, the way
blackberry and cedar shoots wait
for meadow burnings, noticing

in the morning the filmy scrims
of dreams on the catcher, listening
for the flit of wings.

Thinking of her Mother

The banded clouds sliding east
on this brilliant morning braid
silver garlands across blue
winter ridgetops, cool

the force field of rage I feed
on most days as it crackles around
my electric blue Toyota. It
settles a little more as I notice

a woman brushing the tail
of a sixteen-hand gelding as she
thinks of her mother brushing
a ten-year-old's hair,

fifty polled Herefords grazing
in a still life by a placid stream
that could have been painted
in any century,

fumble behind in the back seat
for that innocence my daughters
used to banter back there, that
moving together, that delight.

That Hideous Strength

No one knows why the once
husky man had become nothing
but a crooked stick

inside a tattered coat or why
he stopped before he reached
the top of the hill and flung

his duffeled burden in the dust
or how he got that hideous strength
or if he ever had a holy purpose.

More than the Stock Phrases

It's no bother
when she insisted on cleaning
up after making supper

A penny saved...
when he suggested that they
go out for dinner sometime

It was her mask of equanimity
he found most cloying. In the
evenings she would pick up

her knitting, often unraveling
it by bedtime, when they
retreated to the sanctuary of

their own rooms. To the day
she left it bedeviled him: where
to find the lock to her heart,

where he'd hidden the key.

Signs of Continued Embodiment

Inexactly repeated efforts at connection
with others who recognize the name

The name that came down from my father
along a lineage strewn with suicide

Suicide as a graceful exit from unbearable
heaviness mingled with smaller things

Smaller things like fingernail clippers, like
moldy photographs, like longing.

Cups of Comfort

What if I eased grief
into an armchair by the fire
and handed it a glass of Glenfiddich?

What if I reframed doom
so that time became a friend
and vertigo was mere giddiness?

I don't have the stamina
for so much misery anymore
so I won't recite the full litanies

of suffering in Palestine
in Uttar Pradesh in Ukraine
in the Delta in any of the hearts

of the hated. What if I just
give over to pouring out cups
of comfort, flagons of compassion?

A Spoonful of the Honey

I dreamed I was in love
but the name escaped
the catcher's web, leaving

only the original hot spark
and a spoonful of the honey
that an unknown ancestor

had squeezed from our
old failures. It did not feel
like the romances you read

about, no galloping off on
steeds or tearing off of
clothing, just a lingering

sparkling, and a sweetness.

I Lift the Well Cover

The pileated woodpecker alights
in the black walnut tree, inclines
his sovereign head, flies off
toward the river.

In noonish languor buzzards wheel
in the northerly wind, slow
to the point of insolence; the holdout
maples blaze in the stillness.

I sense a power that will not rise,
an eye that will not seek mine; I lift
the well cover and holler down
for the boy I left behind.

Bluejay in Black Walnut Tree

You are quiet on the branch,
nibbling at the tender tips
of the green shoots pointing
nowhere but upward to blue.

Nothing at all is mentioned
about any viruses ravaging
your gizzard or about
the vortex driving you south
or any of that; and yet

You are so unlike yourself,
uncharacteristically disinclined
to hector the lesser birds,
that I wonder whether
an awakening has occurred,

Whether you might have heard
an inkling of something opening,
rousing so many other beings
that the silence breaks down,
leaving us speechless, blinking.

Only When I Looked Down

Squall line hangs in the north, verga
or riverine not yet revealed, only a
darkening weight pressing down.

If there is only light, then there is
no light; everyone is blind, everything
the same.

Only when I looked down, hyperventilating,
into the depths of my boyhood lake
did I see in the primal mud

Lilies putting down roots, and only by
surrendering to that blackness am I
free to float in the sun all day,

And when I found the salmon lily blossom,
the luminous pink of my endoscoped
bowel walls soothed that final fear.

This Teetering Poem

This teetering poem looks back at me
        the way   the redtail
        found me   in its gaze
        called me   to witness
Spruces two days dead on the road
        from the   snow bomb
        waiting on   a chainsaw
        for hewing   of sinews
Kudzu vines brown breeze blown
        cut to the   root crowns
        by my   machete's
        cold   killer hand
Drought refugee father drowned
        face down   his arm
        around a   diapered child
        in the   Rio Grande
My tired old body spine splayed
        on stone   I found
        that bone   this breath
        all I own

The Itch of Doubt

There must be a pattern
to their honking, deep into
the night, afloat on the pond
to avoid coyote and fox, but
my midnight mind is a thin
broth of sensation and
impression, not yet congealed
into morning's day-blind jello,
a heavier stuff that admits to
nothing but its own certainty,
spending the rest of the day
pretending not to notice
the itch of doubt that rises
when the geese execute
their squadron precision
liftoff, voices and wings in
a unison bent on their one
life mission, and are gone.

The Flutter of an Eyelash

It is midmorning; the emails
have stopped coming. The meeting
was canceled. The deadline was
pushed to the end of next week.

Your better half is off to town.
The birds are listless at the feeder.
The flutter of an eyelash is an event.
You are left to choose.

Resentment or gratitude.
Forethought of grief or sweet
remembrance. Sitting in restless
aliveness in this moment or
lumbering to the kitchen, bent
on the chocolate chips you hid
from yourself. Laughing at your
daily failures. Wasting your life
in delight.

In a Darkened Bedroom

There may be some who do not admit
to that imposter feeling, that need
to be seen only in that certain light,
living in denial of that racking doubt.

I have yet to meet such a one, though
perhaps I did, but I suspect their mask
had not yet cracked and left them
in a darkened bedroom, weeping.

These Holdout Beech Leaves

What if the abacus was not about counting things
but about keeping our beliefs from vanishing?

What if the scream of the red tailed hawk
that startles me from that dreamy bardo state

between annihilation and a more beautiful life
is only to distill what I love into a single sound?

And now that astrophysicists have made ripples
in gravity perceptible, what do I make of these

holdout beech leaves fluttering in winter wind?

A Walk into Darkness

It's harder to rise before dawn in the summer,
and some bird has usually beaten me to it,

but if I aim to survive this murderous heat
I will need to hit the pause button on the tape

player that is my mind lest the usual excuses
loop and loop and loop: too tired, too humid,

too many joint aches, too many temptations
calling from the fridge. But on this morning,

I knock around under the bed for those boots,
draw on the smart wool socks, slip out the

door designed to hold back my exuberance,
and step out one more time into darkness.

I am Just a Flick of a Tail

In amniotic water
as the asexual Asian carp
vegetarian leviathan
lures me to dive
into a place I cannot
        breathe,

When all this time
I had denied in the mud
        of memory
        the gills
I wore for my mother
in that time outside
        of time
        when I was
the water and the fish
and the swimming,

So that now the thrashing
breach the carp makes
when my canoe breaks
its basking on the surface
        of the pond
        becomes the shudder

Of that wave rippling out
from this singular motion
        touching
        every pulsing thing.

Your Life is Only This

Two hummingbirds
vie in needle ferocity
for the nectar at the
red speckled feeder

Jason's guitar weeps
for the binges he left
behind when his soul
finally spoke up

These clouds impress
a gray ceiling over
this green canopy
which was dark enough

A death wish glides by
in a murder of crows
skimming the periphery
of this beautiful life

A presence vacillates
in the field by the pond
where reclusive fishes
inspire one more breath

Loon Requiem

This tiny lake takes in the dying hemlock
falling imperceptibly into its arms

as the lake bottom darkness gives over
to a softness felt in dreams,

sending up from the same black roots
hails of hyacinths and lilies.

We laze on the surface, but only the loon
brings up the life-giving fishes, only

the black-headed one sings in the places
where light fails in wintering southern

oceans, flight plumage stripped away,
pale dun feathers losing the holy name,

leaving only the long knife of the beak,
the red circle of the eye for hunting

in the hopeless waters of January storms
that do not darken our dog day dreams.

Year after year we struggle to remember
on summer nights the summoning power

of the loon's call, to restore these beloveds
lost to us underneath this feathered grace.

Awakening in an ALS journey

Only now does the ability to exhale
become so precious to these alveoli
biosacs not sleeping even in darkness
breathing in what becomes our light

Light that begins as nothing but air
drawn down night-blinded tubes
tubes that will not admit darkness
past their day-blinded branches

Branches that lead only to smaller
tubules sidewalks and doorsteps
that end at the thinnest of walls
between the living and the dead

The dead who no longer need
the air that was so precious just
the moment before the power was shut off
and the tenant moved out.

A Drop of Water

I cannot destine myself any more
than I can cling to the beliefs that
were planted by advertisers during
the American Dream years of the
1950s. That Leave it to Beaver life
was a sand painting that monks
spent holy months making, then
with holy intention destroyed it.

I do sometimes ask my relations
to place a thumb or an eyebrow
on the invisible compass that
I want to believe points my way
forward to some Avalon, some
place of reunion that was being
prepared for me all these years.

As beliefs fall away like tools
from a rotting canvas belt, I have
nothing left but these odd strings
of words I had not thought of till
just now, held together with
something like the tension that
makes a drop of water for a still
moment be a globe of perfection.

Words that Vanish

How well I remember that night:
What I had believed was a wall
was actually a curtain, or a veil.

It had stood for six decades until
one night my thumb accidentally
touched its blue velvet veneer.

It rippled away, revealing a scene
so splendid that words vanished
like a stream off a ledge in dry air.

Lessons

    i.   *outside*

I've learned that I have to extirpate
Russian olive roots because the cut
stumps will just grow back.

I've learned that rolling my cuffs will
cool my arms while the collared shirt
protects my neck from melanoma.

    ii.   *inside*

I'm learning to dare myself to start to
say things quickly before the egoic
engine of self-doubt can fire up.

I want to learn to watch summer winds
billow these oak leafed limbs in this
searing heat without weeping.

How to Make an Orchestra into a Combo

When I allow the news of the world
into my forebrain through filters made
by others, the Maestro of the orchestra
of the mind is all slash and staccato.

When I tune instead to the frequency
just inside the breath, doves can be heard
cooing, warblers singing a quiet groove
rolling in rhythm with my exhalations.

If I Only Let it Go

Again and again, I ask why
I had to leave home.

Perhaps there were questions
I had not yet heard.

Perhaps I only had to walk
into this ancient grove,

lungs of the world, so I could
breathe easily enough

to remember that I am already
and always home inside

this breath, if I only let it go.
I expect to leave some papers

behind when these lungs
give out, hoping that someone

who reads those words will
only have to release a breath

to find their self home again.

Someone You Have Never Seen

"El ojo que ves no es (the eye you see is not
ojo porque tu no veas; an eye because you see it;
es ojo porque te ve." it is an eye because it sees you.)

—Antonio Machado

In the moments before waking
when the wrens start singing,
in the moments after walking
by old trees on older mosses,

glimpses may start to flicker
in the peripheral of your seeing
of another, someone who has
known you all your dreary life,

someone you have never seen
because the vision you longed for
all these years, wandering blind
across a dead planet of darkest

basalt, wind-up crows, android
lilacs, was with you all that time;
and now that you see this marvelous
other, these same eyes now see you

for the first time, even though
you have awakened in this bed
thousands of times, even though
you have walked these woods

every day for years, so that now
your guest stands beaming at your
door, holding bread, giving wine,
saying now let us feast on this life.

Ancient Revelations

Progress Report to Black Elk

Last night in the silences between barred owl calls
I thought I heard some people passing by the pond.

Might have been plangent minor chords of bullfrog
and fowler's toad sounding a bit like human voices,

but I thought I heard Cherokee forced westward, or
was it Monacan disappearing into the high coves?

I thought I heard bluegill or maybe perch rising to
the surface to feed, but maybe it was only the sound

of four hundred years of weeping. There were no
tracks this morning, but winter is coming so today

I left out on the trail leading west from the ridge
line where you can see the mountains some small

packets of poems written on lichen, bound up
with braided sweetgrass, left out on mossed stones.

Remnant Revenants of Recurrent Dreams

Monacan leaf trails erupting through asphalt parking lots

Mosses holding moisture for returning bison stampedes

Three-eared dioxin babies swarming out of white steel cribs

Jaguar palimpsests packing .22s to clear out the Pantanal

Cattle rustler liana wraiths braiding up from the stream valleys

Small voices deafening up from Red Cloud Oglala school basement

Ishtar>>Tiamat>>Kali>>Nemesis megachurch wrecking crew

Tiny matchboxes slipped into twenty million pockets for the bonfires

That will raise the Innocent from the ashheaps that will dream us back into harmony

Whalebone Necklace

When the solo girl living
out with the tundra deer sang,
her family's kayaks found
the safe eddies in the river
where the fat fish waited.

When the girl sang radiant
songs in the original tongue,
the white whales swam
farther up the river, a few
giving themselves to the bears.

When the girl sang in her
chaste way out of motherhood,
the fever left her little brother
so he could become the hunter
his father needed him to be.

When the girl sang grieving
lullabies that calmed the bears
at the side of the dying chief
the elders were so moved
they buried her beside him.

When the grave was revealed
after two hundred generations
her bones were wrapped in furs,
a whalebone necklace sagged
through the empty space where

A song once gave rise to a river.

Animacy in Wild Strawberry

Puhpowee is Potawotami
for the power and really
the longing that pushes
the capped mushroom
mycelium spore messenger
into the open air overnight.

Is like the force coming through
    Dylan Thomas' green fuse
connecting the blossom to appendages
    of pollinators
who want only the nectar
but carry the pollen for free.

Yawe was Potawotami for being
long before the Israelites
    were breathed
    into that dream life
by the great white father
is now and always only as simple
    as the sweetness
    of the wild strawberry.

Yawe is being in that moment
before the next inhalation
when life decides which corpses
    are not ready
leaving we the still breathing
    astonished
    as our only life
rises in our chests.

Consonance and Assonance and All
—inspired by a Sami (arctic indigenous tribe) music recording

In this Sami singing way
the 'n's bend into the flow
        become river banks
        and the roots
that hold back the banks
become the stones
        in the water
only to help the water
        sing and in that way
become another tongue
        that sings the river.

These 'n's grown long, their tops
        softened to vowels,
        become ancient horns,
        too long to be held
        up by human hands,
resting their bended ends
        on the frozen ground
as if the earth wants to place
        its bass coloring
        into the notes
that no craftsman's hand
could ever bend into being.

News of the Great Turning

Three Lessons in Survival for this Century

    i.

Don't spend so long dickering with stones to persuade them
to come down from the mountain, to border your hydrangea,

or grow new moss over lichen, because this is their journey
into soil and to the sea. Make the fire circle where they are,

listen to them speak with their gravity against your gloves,
become quiet enough to pick up some of their equanimity.

Listen to your aching spine, your pounding heart, give in
to their ancient opinion. Sit still on them as their gift to you.

    ii.

Use this leisure to watch hummingbirds hover, take note of
how their featherings merge color and sound into one motion,

see their twirling tails make the whole web shimmer in sheer
determination. If you can, climb two miles high in the Andes,

notice how much longer they rest between nectarings, observe
how at night, their bodies cool and their hearts slow to almost

nothing, yet in the next day's sun they are back at it, wasting
no time in finding the petals and the pistils of the holy nectar.

    iii.

These birds don't question the verdicts of gravity, weather, or
the human tornado as it engulfs them. They do not brood or

trouble their lives with forethought of grief, so don't worry,
they will simply show up in some new country, beaks bending
into some novel heliconia, hearts beating to the new temperature,

wasting no time cursing their new conditions, remain nothing
but beak and feather, fiercely focused on the flower's nectar.

Planting Words

Time was monsters came from the north,
Yeti and Wetigo and the others that elders
invoked when the young people argued

and talked sass and interrupted parents
in midsentence. *Don't make me say this
twice* they were admonished. And now

the beasts come from the south on sticky
winds that flap the wilting leaves, extend
their ruthless tendrils into our very hearts,

planting words like concertina wire fences:
Mexican, communist, heat wave, hurricane.

Naked Blind Sweeties

The mouse in my firewood rack
deserves the same blessing
as any of my dear ones, even
as she shreds the New York
Review of Books I was counting
on for kindling starter. I wish
now that I could restore that
feathered nest, built by hand
to hold some small number
of naked blind sweeties,
trusting the mother to bend
all the forces of nature to
provide a single safe, warm
shelter from all this ravening.

Knowing of the Soot

The trees that soar above the terrace
hickory sweetgum poplar oak
accept squirrels, accept woodpeckers,
accept bark beetles, accept wind
and rain and wildfire. If you believe
they are not intelligent, I will not
squabble, will not try to compress
their millions of years of knowledge
to our few thousand, will gratefully
accept their shelter, their dead leaves,
their hard nuts, knowing of the soot
and clay and humous that in a few
trips around the sun we will become.

A Flat File Across a Mattock Blade

If this earth is my hospice nurse
then as I breathe, I will be hers.

I move among trees long felled
by age or rot or insect or fungi

and those that would be felled
by these vines that will not relent,

their plumed festooned foliage
shuttered only for the winter,

unless someone like me rasps
a flat file across a mattock blade

and ambles into a hardwood glade.

Garnets

I'd like to believe
I'm evolving albeit
faster than Darwin.

I'd like to believe
I am not a noun or
a verb, a knowing,

a hovering presence
that could speak any
thing, do nothing,

except for the hard
edges that snag the
soul in the predawn,

garnets darkening in
my pores as they go
drier and drier in

this terrible heat.

To See the Hummingbird

If it wasn't so dry, steam
would rise off my shoulders,

which otherwise are merely
a lintel for my marvelous head.

If the heat wasn't such a blast
furnace, I would do better at

standing up straight, but I have
stopped keeping score, stopped

shouting into this pitiless wind,
accepted our fatal mistake, wait

only to see if the hummingbird
still flits to the fake red feeder.

The New Normal

In Chiapas Mexico howler monkeys
are falling from trees with heat stroke.

Last summer my oldest friend's nephew
died on a 115-degree street in Phoenix,

unable to crawl out of his twenty-year
addiction. So many of us grow tired of

living in this riddle of extremes, where
both choices are unacceptable, that we

stop taking action altogether, become
addicted to word games on our phones,

allow numbness to become normalcy.

This Kitchen Remains Quiet

This winter wind winnows the last
leaves clinging to the gutter guards,

soughing loudly in the crowns that
this planet is still alive under the rush,

in the quiet beneath the storm surge
wave crest, even as we count the losses

in human reckonings, still clinging to
the belief that technology and reason

are sufficient to stay the ruination, no
matter how unflinching the winds ^^

waves ^^ wildfires ^^ droughts remain.
This kitchen remains quiet but for the

rhythmic chopping of carrots, turnips,
onions, and the mincing of cumin,

cardamom, coriander, their aromas
converging to prod these covid-dulled

taste buds back to life. Into this stew
I stir my dried failures, jarred hopes.

The Bangladesh School of Resilience

What if the weight of doom
from all the terrible statistics
bloating the sack of dread
in your belly
was only a habit of mind?

What if the bent-armed woman
carrying her child in choking
Dhaka traffic was there only
to change your dread
to compassion?

What if the rickshaw puller
proud on his sequined rainbow
garlanded in the swelter of the
Old City street is simply showing
you how resilient pride looks?

What if the crowd gathering
around the only *Amrikans*
in that old Mughul fort whipped
out their phones only to change
your panic to joy as we leaned
into each other's selfies?

News of the World

Dispatches from the Levant

i.   *from the Kibbutz*

The morning after the shots
        and the screams
we dared not go to the mailbox,
        fearing to be seen.
They had tried and failed to pry
        our door open;
we kept the children extra quiet
        in the safe room
by handing out the dozen lemon
cookies we had left a quarter
        piece at a time,
        making a game
of who could chew them and
then sip their raw goat's milk
        most inaudibly.

ii.   *from the Hospital*

We gathered the surviving plurality
        of our family
        in the basement
where the building's possible collapse
        might not be fatal.
Yasmin drew our dear little ones
        Nadia and Iman and Amir
        to her in silence
because their eardrums were damaged
        by the explosions.
She had hoped that my cousin Omar's
        portable charger
would let her get through to her mother
        in Turkey,
but the connector was incompatible with
        her useless phone.

Lumbering to the Capitol

In Rip Van Winkle's world
the soundtrack of summer storms
was made by thunder beings.

Then he woke up, and by asking
neighbors came to understand
that his world had vanished.

What must it have been like
to hear such dour epiphanies,
the death of one's divinities?

It's hard to pick from the options:
maybe it's like seeing Indian
culture erased in white schools;

or seeing a dustbowl farmer's
faith in weather's mercy dried up
and blown away; or watching

the parade of a wizard with a mane
of flame lumbering to the capitol
ringleading a circus of darkness.

Enthusing with a Glee Undimmed

The flutter of your rectangle in this Zoom
universe signals the translucence some old
people take on, revealing lights of medicine
wheel quartz and old campfires burning
through the emaciation of your identity.

In this chameleon space the cumulus clouds
piling up sunset radiant over the blue ridge
outshine your eyes, faded now to blinking
portals to whatever's playing, autumn foliage
or greenstone walls or blue heron at the pond.

It's time to shake off these interpretations; new
colors are gelling behind your eyes as they
pale, as your skin reveals blue veins beneath,
as you become a docent enthusing with a glee
undimmed an advertisement for the next world.

I Pray that Your Ammunition Runs Out before Dark

as your semiautomatic fire echoes over the lake.

I can wait, as nuthatch and kingfisher
chitter their business, as the hemlock
cathedral up the hill cradles
the evening light unshaken.

I wonder what comes later, whether
your adrenals are this exhausted, your
eardrums this numb from the assault
on those tender places.

After dinner I pray the pine duff built up
on the forest floor will make a bower
for your terror, and give you rest.

The Truck Driver on my Tail

i.
cannot hear these hickory nuts
falling through leaves
of poplar, oak, sweet gum;

may be late for another day
at work dozing the red clay
of another forested hillside

so that people with the money
can get their Blue Ridge views,
from their Trex decks, holding

wine in sky-opening glasses.

ii.
If I could be made the good cop
I would pull him over, take him
out for coffee, ask him if he has

heard much from his kids lately or
if his lumbar disc has stopped
bulging or whether Oxycodone

is harder to get now. Even if he
only grunted, I still might place
him in a cell draped in fine cloth

with a bed so warm that his mother
appears in the night, brushing his brow
with a hand so soft that he cannot

writhe off its tenderness any longer.

A Field of Cloud Mysteries

or perhaps a material darker
than the white pines
behind the house
or a terribly small thing*
that lives in a field inside
the meadow we bush-hog
every year so these risen things
can greet each other's solitudes,
milkweed to aster,
beak of meadowlark
to snout of vole; or perhaps

it is a field visible only
through cloud mysteries
in the great curve circling for miles
under Alpine stone; hurling
everything we know as equations
into collisions hoping if nothing
more to regain
the joy of smelling
the blue spruces'
sweet dark cones.

---

*Peter Higgs is a Scottish physicist whose 1960s work posited the existence of the Higgs Boson, aka the "God particle," thought to be fundamental to all mass in the universe. After 2012 experiments at the particle accelerator beneath the Swiss Alps confirmed Higgs' theory, he was awarded the Nobel Prize in 2013.

Stafford's Last Year: Cento

Old mistakes come calling: no life
happens just once. Whatever snags
even the edge of your days will abide.
You are a turtle with all the years on your back.

Maybe people have to go in and out of shadows
till they learn that floating, that immensity;
maybe somebody has to explore what happens
when one of us wanders over near the edge.

Whatever fits will be welcome, whatever
steps back in the fog will disappear…
It's heavy to drag, this big sack of what
you should have done.

And now if there is any light at all
it knows how to rest on the faces of friends.
Touches of wind. The room you have
in the world is ready to change.

Will you ever bring a better gift for the world
than the breathing respect that you carry
When you turn around, starting here, lift this
new glimpse that you found.

Well, it was yesterday. And the sun came,
Why
It came.

Sources: lines selected from poems written by William Stafford in 1993, the last year of his life. The last three lines end the poem he wrote the day he died. All selections from *The Way It Is*.

Confessional Revelations

That Fluttering Spirit

My first family revelation came to me
when I was thirteen. After my father's
rage sent us off in the green Chevy
station wagon into the night,
my mother driving too fast, telling us
of his father's suicide attempt, of my
sister's crib death before I was born,
I didn't have the words but knew that
my innocence had reached its end.

My second family revelation came to me
when I was nineteen. She was bedridden
over Christmas, then took off on a manic
rocket that crashed her life in six chaotic
years. There were other breaches in the
veil of our normalcy, but I recall these
as the first doors to the demimonde that
was kept from us in school and on TV.

But there was that TV airing of Peter Pan.
My father later told me that they named
the first three of us Peter, Wendy, and
Michael from that play, as if our family
came from Neverland, but when Betsey
died, they folded that show. Yet I keep
my hold on the theory that if enough of us
clap, really clap, from the heart, we can
bring that fluttering spirit back to life.

A Poem in which my Grandfathers meet Lorca

i.
Victor, an original Mad Man who confessed
Later after giving it all to God that he spent
His career trying to get people to buy
Things they didn't need and couldn't
Afford. On a Tuesday night in a speakeasy
On 52nd Street Lorca buys him three
Gin and tonics, gets him drunk on the night air
Of Granada, softening the brutality
Of the Depression, easing Victor
Out of his new religion. He moves Elsie
And the three girls to Spain; my mother marries
A Grenadine guitarist whose arpeggios form
An oasis for the heart of her bipolar, and I am
Writing this at sunset from my veranda.

ii.
Ned, who decided to become a stockbroker
In 1928, found by his 12-year-old son
With his head in the oven in 1929. Lorca
Takes the New Haven Railroad up to visit
Him in the sanitarium where the men in white
Coats took him that night. A Jasmine aroma,
Or a nightingale's call, slips into that locked
Room on the universal tongue, as the poet,
Speaking almost no English, uses the honey
Of words to melt those layers of capitalist
Despair. Ned becomes a chain-smoking
Detective novelist, his son doesn't
Have to be the man of the family anymore,
Sails the Sound with his cousin Seymour,
Selling their handbuilt sloops, reaching before
A running sea, tacking into a freshening elation.

Parallax[1] Revealed Beneath Princess Pine

At the big conference I once longed to attend
I stepped back into a shadow and vanished

The cowboy wallpaper of my childhood room
became a palimpsest at the bottom of the pool

Eliot went from the titan on the mountain to
our humble condition of complete simplicity

The goddess my lusty boy sensed in the laurel
grove keeps winning at her scrabble by the fire

The princess pine I picked in the woods behind
the house became the kudzu that kills my poplars

The birds I shot with my air rifle the fire fading
from their eyes feast at the feeder in winter sun

The mycelium I never noticed conspires with
tree roots to teach me all I now need to know

The golden child my mother's redeemer returns
as the great grandchildren she never got to meet

-

---

[1] "the observed displacement of an object caused by the change of the observer's point of view"

If Minerva Shrugged

Or any of the old goddesses,
and the babies stopped coming,
no one would catch me as I fall
unnoticed into senescence, not only
the linearity of time breaking up, and
putting the faces of others on my
familiars, but conflating this
fresh-painted place with my
childhood private Avalon,
where I insist on believing
I will wind up regardless, though
I will not recognize the place,
for there is no one now to hold
my hand, the way my sister did
on the first day of grade school,
those hard-floor harsh-lit halls
booming with stentorian tones
of Principal Goodfield who first
taught me to fear my own voice,
doubt my own instincts, clamp
a stone cover on my birthright
        well of elation.

What I Didn't Know

I was raised to stay in my lane
though not many roads had lanes
all nicely marked with double
yellow lines let alone the rumble
strips and the little reflectors like
roadkill staring back in the dark.

I was also taught by schoolmates
not to step on a crack for fear of
breaking my mother's back though
six children and losing one and then
the bipolar eruption was more than
enough to throw her into the abyss.

No one told me how chili peppers
could make you weep or about Chile
how the secret police would jump
from their vans, lean you against
a wall, put a bullet in your head,
make you into a desaparecido.

Mother's Day Pantoum

My mother is stuck in monochrome,
a Dorothea Lange forties photograph:
my sister on her hip before our home
turned into the scene for her epitaph.

A Dorothea Lange forties photograph
like a thousand other women's faces,
still scenes that may serve as epitaphs,
unsure if they will sleep in safe places.

So like a thousand other women's faces
I almost forgot the way she came apart,
or what it felt like to sleep in safe places
as I hid out in wait for my life to start.

Too well I remember her coming apart:
her manic rambling before Margaret Mead
sent me deeper into hiding, refusing to start,
God knew where the 70s were going to lead.

If only her ramblings before Margaret Mead
had found a sure cure in cocktails or meds,
if an inscrutable God had cast me as the lead
in my play, I might not have acted so dead.

But I get to choose the photographs I keep:
sister still on hip, someone else is home;
and though that pain still darkens my sleep,
My mother ages well in this monochrome.

Posthumous Instructions to my Brother Michael

Forget the lung damage. Forget
the radiation. Forget the malignant
mass under your sternum competing
with your trachea for oxygen.

Try to forget your grade school rage,
and my artful provocation, stealing
your sombrero full of chestnuts
or your warped tennis racket.

See if you can forget the dart in
your scalp, or that you were standing
so close to that colored-wedge cork
target, to that bullseye so black.

If you can, forget your dyslexic
Moaning in the next room while I
wandered diffidently, obediently
into the merit scholar bullseye.

Don't forget that your wife kicked
you out. Remember it was because
you followed our mother into
that bad-weather bipolar bullseye.

I won't forget the amazing grace
of your new love and your new
faith, or the gravelly gratitude
you found fifty years too late.

You never forgot in these last
years to call me on my birthday
every single time, leaving those
nutty singing voicemail messages.

Forget it, just forget it, for I will
remember you until this body too
gives out, lugging these images
over the gravel of my own road.

My Daughter's New Home

This hundred acre wood
though devoid of Pooh and Roo
is a department store of diversity
from the restored prairie camas
and lupine to the wetland rails
and redwing blackbirds to
the douglas firs standing here since
before the Hudson's Bay Company.

Each of their bodies is as fragile
as the mosquito I crush as I sit
quietly on the cottage porch.
Together they make a subtle web
that includes Tahoma, so stately
in the east, an icebound cauldron
of ancient fire, patient, waiting.

What about the Year I Turned 18

What about that James Earl Ray
That murderer of Martin Luther King
And how about that LBJ stepping down
Just a few days before how ya like that

What about those plucky Vietnamese
Unleashing hell on a holiday Tet they say
And how about them cocky Americans
Not admitting they were losing a war

What about that June what about that Bobby
Kennedy killed just before my graduation
And how about that light fading from his eyes
On that concrete hotel kitchen floor

What about that speech that valedictory
I was supposed to give what about learning
How to live before figuring how to make
A living what about that first failed raid

On the inarticulate what about that shabby
Equipment unable to find words for that moment
What about Dick Daley and the Chicago pigs
And Tricky Dick and the best musicians

Overdosing and the rest of us descending
Into that numbness not knowing what it was
What about that how about it what was it
Who was I then and who am I to be now

What about the best once again lacking
All conviction what about the worst even fuller
Of passionate intensity torches on our grounds
Killing with their muscle cars on our streets

And how about that fat pumpkin-haired cartoon
Making Nixon look like an honorable man
What about them skinheads spewing the hatred
Our fathers fought that we might be spared

How about it America what about that shadow
Problem what about that denial problem how
About that projection problem your blaming
Of the other how about it you righteous ones

What about those Russian hackers learning
That sliming Hillary made better money
Greased on reactivity stinking up democracy
How about that Vlad how about it Don

How about that internet thing whipping up
Resentment like baited barbecue sauce mixed
With that gasoline tossed on those charring corpses
What about that my man-child how about that

How about that red meat for the resentful red meat
For men who will not eat that same old shadow
How about that half century of not learning a thing
How about we admit it America how about that?

University Village: Etudes

i.
The pink weight of dawn
pushes down the blue
············edge of night
············making the lights
of the retirement home
on the ridge over the river
············glitter copper.

Anne is back in Johnstown,
January 1945, curled up
with the radio voice of Roosevelt,
············avuncular honey flowing
············from the big brown
Philco in the empty living room.
Still no word from Derek
············with the Screaming Eagles
············in the Ardennes Forest.

In her state of mind the staff agree
············not to try
to explain to her that the Nazis
············are back.
The unfiltered sun through
the floor-length windows
is fierce enough and merciful
············enough to sear
············her memory shut.

ii.
On the ridge over the river
the retirement home windows
············glow copper
············again in the dawn
as the breastplate of Hector
must have shone while he waited
············for Achilles.

Hank drifts in and out of the same
dream of the slender Japanese boy,
      more like a girl,
      really, the one
he bayonetted behind the beach
      on Saipan
      after Ernie
took it in the belly from the kid's
machine gun.

His daughter is bringing the grandkids
      for lunch. Zack
in fifth grade is obsessed with WWII
      weaponry of all kinds,
wants to know if the machine gun
      was Type 11
      or Type 21.

iii.
Though the windows of my father's
New Jersey Sunrise room never glowed
      copper at dawn,
or if they did he would not have seen
      such glory
from his wheelchair inside, perhaps

he dreamt of his summer honeymoon
      of 1940,
sailing the Bay on the True Love
      with my mother,
or was it of that girl he knew in school?

Or the sleepy San Juan Sunday
when the chief petty officer ran up
      waving a telegram
saying Pearl Harbor had been bombed,
      he wondering
'where the hell Is Pearl Harbor?'

Or the boredom of tug escort duty
circling the old tub over and over,
       as perhaps he protected
       us, steadily
and at a distance, the ensign furling
itself around the mast, he reversing course
       to unfurl the flag
         one more time?

Apologizing to Ferlinghetti

You never took
              the deal
the hand
     America dealt

what did   you have
to lose   anyway
father   and mother
      dead or
                    gone mad

you spoke   French first
     so why not   bat the English
words   way out there
fungoes of the mind

screw the form   screw the State
just write

and how you wrote
wrote and sold   sold like hell

turned on the Lights   published
Howl   screwed the Court
didn't thank   the Academy
     that did shit for you

just invited everyone
to the party
coffeehouse hipsters
     the dharma dumpsters
     full of books
the Academy kept   throwing out

your bookstore rambled right
         past the millenium
giving my friend   Jan
time   to finally   get the guts
                         walk up
to the counter   speak to
the slacker at the register   say sorry
slip him a ten spot   for the book

she stole   in 1970

Acknowledgments

"This Kitchen Remains Quiet", "Finding the Lost Boy Before Dark", "A poem in which my grandfathers meet Lorca", "Dispatches from the Levant" and "A Flat File Across a Mattock Blade" were previously published in *The Sandy River Review*.

"Apologizing to Ferlinghetti" was published in *Streetlight Magazine.*

"That Comet You Glimpsed", "She Sews a Blue Silk Lining", and "The White Plastic Basket" were published in *The Journal of the Virginia Writers Club.*

"I Left the Well Cover" was previously published in Tupelo Press's *Thirty Days*

Bill Prindle is deepening his voice in the third half of life. His poetry explores the seams between the human and nonhuman worlds, working to forge a new reciprocity that restores heart to our mutual life. Drawing on his experience wandering in forests, using plant medicine, driving on American highways, practicing restorative agriculture on his five acres, and learning to shift his attention from the world he fears to the one he wants, his poetry is both personal and collective, introspective and prophetic, reminiscent and present.

He is inspired by many poets, of all ages, races, genders, and beliefs. But as someone writing as a white male, in a body nearing the end of its earthly journey, he confesses his reliance for inspiration on dead white men. Such as Yeats (excerpted from *Sailing to Byzantium*):

> *An aged man is but a paltry thing,*
> *A tattered coat upon a stick, unless*
> *Soul clap its hands and sing, and louder sing*
> *For every tatter in its mortal dress*

Or Eliot (from *The Four Quartets*):

> *As we grow older the world becomes stranger, the pattern more*
>   *complicated*
> *Of dead and living. Not the intense moment isolated, with no before*
>   *and after,*
> *But a lifetime burning in every moment…*
> *Old men ought be explorers…*
> *We must be still and still moving*
> *Into another intensity*
> *For a further union, a deeper communion*

He has won multiple Poetry Society of Virginia awards, and has been published in Verse-Virtual, Streetlight Magazine and its 2021 anthology, Sandy River Journal, Tupelo Press' Thirty Days anthology, the Written River Journal, and the What Rough Beast journal. He has studied with Lisa Russ Spahr, Neil Perry, Gregory Orr, Sharon Olds, and C.K. Williams. He lives with his wife in the woods near Charlottesville, Virginia.

www.ingramcontent.com/pod-product-compliance
Lightning Source LLC
Chambersburg PA
CBHW030055170426
43197CB00010B/1530